Party, Sex & Drugs

"A Teenagers Survival Guide"

Author:
Nesa Kovacs

Party, ^Sex^ & Drugs
"A Teenagers Survival Guide"

Copyright © 2011 by Nesa Kovacs
Cover Design by: Laura Shinn
Formatted by: Laura Shinn
ISBN-13: 978-0-615-51914-2
ISBN-10: 0615519148
LCCN: 2011937955

A Little Publishing Company books may be ordered through booksellers or by contacting:

A Little Publishing Company
Hollywood, CA
www.alittlepublishingcompany.com
1-240-350-9234

Because of the nature of the Internet, any web addresses or links contained in this book may have changed since publication and may no longer be valid.

The views expressed in this work are solely those of the author and do not necessarily reflect the views of the publisher, hereby disclaims any responsibility for them.

Thank you

Wow...this may take a moment since this is my very first book!

My personal thanks goes to many people I feel that have been influential in my short life span thus far. People come in and out of your life and some stay and some go, but the ones that leave their imprint on my heart and soul are the ones I salute and say thank you to.

The list starts here:

My mom: You are my rock, you are my friend, you are my soul, and I am a mini-me of you. Not sure if that is good or bad, but either way I thank you for letting me be me.

My Dad: You always stayed on my case and made sure I had a fair enough relationship with God and I respect you for that. We have a lot of different views on life but I still love you. You're still my favorite dad. Wait, you're my only dad!

The Christies: Wow! You came into my life like a tornado, you could of gave a girl a warning...lol. You were the first that believed in my visions besides my own mom. You took my vision and made it happen and for that, I owe you more than words can say. Thanks to Chani for inspiring me to write my very first book and to create my very own foundation.

Lin Bickelman: *My very first manager in Hollywood. Boy oh Boy...lol. It was a long battle but you hung in there, thanks for offering me a chance to come to Cali and do what I love to do best, simply act.*

Laron Tate & Debbie Holstein: *When I had nowhere to turn and we were lost in LA, you came in the nick of time to be my personal assistants, acting coaches and more. With little money, you guys made it happen for me, you just did. Maybe it was just that Chi-town love we had for one another but regardless you did it. You will always be in my heart.*

Ms. Sheila Baker: *Thank you for throwing me on stage as an emcee without any training, you just believed in me and you still do. You are a hero to the thousands of students you taught in school as a retired teacher, and you are still a hero to the youth of today, and for that I salute you for inspiring us to be somebody in society.*

Candy: *You already know! What you did for me and my mom is priceless! Although you were going through rough times, you never let us go without! You are worth so much more than you think. I will always cherish every day we lived with you, you definitely deserve peace in your life. Oh and thanks for teaching me how to drive at age 12, that was cool!*

Montana: *Thank you for always having my back and being a true friend. When gunshots were flying around us and you covered me at the* age of 14 just on instinct, I knew then this was the kind of friend my mama said I need to have, her famous words are: Know who you rolling with. And trust me, you proved it, thank god that night I was rolling with you!

Pamela Smith: *You were that bank account we never saw coming when we needed it the most…lol! You have helped me & mom since I was a girl in pigtails from New York to LA you have always been family. You will always be a part of us.*

Harvey Walden IV: *For just sticking your neck out for a bunch of teens that you barely knew. For believing in me , my project and the whole team. See you are not so tough after all…I'm just sayin!*

Terrance Howard: *Wow! None of this would be possible without you! When I met you my whole life changed. My belief in me changed. When you told me about the sperm thing I didn't know where you were going with that story, but then it made sense, If I could fight off millions of sperms to attach myself to the egg in my mom's womb and be born, than I can fight for everything I want in life. I got it! Now I fight for everything, I took your advice and created me, created my path, I took control, and my hands will always be on the steering wheel. Thank you, thank you, thank you for not letting me give up! I will treasure you for the rest of my life.*

Taraji P. Henson: *To my home girl from DC, thanks for coming to LA and just killing the game, you had fire, you had belief, you just kept kicking open doors with some real talent. You inspired me to know that I can do it too!*

Irene Grigoriadis: *Thank You for always being there for me and mom since we first moved to Cali and when my brother passed. I hope you will always & truly believe me and moms appreciate you!*

To Miss Chris: *Ms. Detroit, Ms. Prada, & all the finer things in life, this thanks is to you for always having my mama's back and stepping in to help us at a moments' notice. You are our family.*

To Dorothy Dandridge: *Although you are not here in the flesh, not a day that goes by that I don't think of the impact you have had on my life. Since my very first school report in the 4th grade when I did a full report on your life, I knew I wanted to be like you, so here I am in Hollywood, wanting to grow up and be just like you. I want my Walk of Fame star to be near yours. So see ya soon!*

To My Late Uncle Tony: *Thanks for seeing the beauty in me, before anyone else did.*

To My Big Bro Rob: *Stay focused...let's make Chris proud.*

And Finally to my brother Chris: R.I.P. Christopher Kendall Richard whom always told me; **"Don't be like nobody else, be different".**

And I shall be!

A Special Thank you

I would like to thank everyone whom has
been my support throughout my life.

I would like to thank you, the readers
for supporting my dream.

This book would not have been possible without
giving thanks to God. He gave me life and told
me to find my purpose in life, and for that I
thank him for being a part of my life every day.

Nesa Kovacs

Coming Soon:

From Beauty Queen to TV Screen

Party, ^{Sex} and Drugs

Nesa Kovacs
Hollywood California

Party, ^{Sex} & Drugs

CONTENTS

Me and my BFF "Kelli Renee" going to a party!

Chapter 1

The Parties...*what you need to know and what you think you know!*

PARTIES, now that's something that every teen wants to get invited to; a party. Parties are cool for all ages but especially teens, it seems to be the happening thing no matter where you come from or where you may live around the world, it's every kid's dream to get invited to a party especially from the hottest and most popular kids in school.

2

Parties can be fun and of course boring, I mean b-o-r-i-n-g. That means everyone is just sitting around twiddling their thumbs waiting for the bomb to drop to have fun or it could mean for girls, there are no cute boys there...lol. Got to have cute boys or why get all dressed up.

Believe it or not, there are so many different variations of parties that you have to pick and choose from before you can even decide which party is right for you. But one of the other most important decisions is choosing who to go with. Choosing the right friend to party with is just as important as choosing the right party to attend because some friends can lead you to the wrong type of party which actually happened to me.

If I recall I was fourteen years old when I begged my mom to go to my first party, that is, without having the normal family style party where the whole family is there and the kids wind up in the basement or someone's bedroom just playing music and talking and everyone is related to one another.

So finally at age fourteen my mom gave me the "OK" to go to my first grown-up high school party without the family and it was a lot of fun until there was a drive-by. So some of you I 'am sure are asking "What's a drive-by"? Well, let me break it down to you: a drive-by is a urban term for a dark car with dark tented windows where you can't see inside the car and the people in the car drive by a specific street or location to purposely do harm to someone as fire off shot guns at them or throw fire bombs at someone or something, and once they have committed this act of violence they keep driving very fast to get away from the scene, thus calling it a drive-by.

Normally this is some sort of gang related violence that is related to another criminal act and normally happens in urban and Latino low income neighborhoods according to the statistics. So now that you know what a drive-by is, let me tell how it all began.

I was fourteen and I was invited to go to a party in Canoga Park, CA. with one of my older friends Montana. I was so excited and I practically begged my mom to go. I told her it would be ok and that definitely there would be no drama and to make it even sweeter, I promised her that this was going to be a great party, not to worry and I knew all the safe party rules; plus I gave her the cute pouty face and who could say "NO" to that.

5

After mom said it was ok, I put my high heels on, my makeup on, made my hair look like a million bucks, and I was ready to go party. I was absolutely ready for this party and I was ready to be the hottest and prettiest girl there.

So mom and I picked up my friend Montana and we drove to Canoga Park for the party. When we arrived of course, my mom gave us all the "*do not do*" part rules before we got out of the car. We nodded yes to all the rules and said good bye to my mother.

When we walked inside the party, it was popping and of course, I'm scoping out the cute boys. The party was fun and I was having fun too. Everyone was dancing and mingling but for some reason I wanted to go outside to get some fresh air but Montana was still dancing and I didn't want to go outside by myself so I decided to wait until

6

Montana was finished dancing. And, thank god I waited for her because if I hadn't, I would not be alive today to tell you my story.

Right before the dance song ended and while Montana was still dancing, I noticed that the song that was banging loudly through the speakers sounded a little off beat and then all of a sudden a group of people from outside the club rushed in the club in terror.

The next thing I knew my friend Montana grabbed me by my arm and yanked me under a table with her. I didn't know what was going on at the moment but then put two and two together and assumed that since everyone hit the ground, someone must be shooting.

7

We started to hear screams and gunfire and voices from the other party goers that two people had been shot. And right before my very own eyes I saw a teen that had been shot in the back and was being dragged through the club to the bathroom.

And you would think witnessing that would have been enough for me to just pass out, but right after that we heard a banging at the door coming from the outside. Everyone turned their head so fast towards the door and a silence came over the entire club. All you could hear was banging on the door like someone was trying to get in.

Finally someone opened the door and we discovered it was one of the security guards from outside that had been shot in the back. Throughout all of this chaos, Montana still had her arms wrapped around me trying to calm me down; now that's a true friend that has your back. Everyone had to stay down and in hiding until the police arrived for our own safety. I called my mom and told her to rush over as fast as she could.

This party was not a fun party anymore. Montana and I was scared, but all I could think about was my mom. What was she going to say after I spent all week telling her that there was going to be absolutely no drama at this party. My guess is I will probably never be allowed to go to a party again for a very long time. Boy was I wrong about this party, who could have predicted a shooting at my very first grown-up party.

Finally the police showed up and it was time to leave. As we were walking outside the club we had to look down to make sure we weren't stepping in any blood. Thank god my mom was right outside, and the first thing she said was, "I told you so"; and as much as I hated to admit it, mom was right. You can't control everyone's actions and you definitely can't control a party that's not yours.

After that horrible event I decided I wasn't quite ready for that kind of party and I told myself to choose wisely on which parties I go to and more importantly which friend to go with. Now I only attend parties where I am a special invited guest meaning on the V.I.P list where my partying is in the V.I.P room which normally is a more secured and controlled atmosphere, or I simply attend what we call a "Kickback" which is basically close friends getting together in a familiar spot, because witnessing that was one of the biggest eye openers I could ever ask for.

As you can see from my experience, there is plenty of partying going on in the world and

10

each party has their own style and a different kind of crowd.

Totally VIP Ready! Gotta Glam it Up a lil'!

12

In case you are not sure what type of party is right for you let me give you the hippest trend of parties that are out there today:

THE HOUSE PARTY - The house party is a party in a house with most likely no parent supervision. This party comes with lots of drinks to include alcohol, beer bongs and socks on the door, which means DO NOT ENTER! Some house parties also have a smoking section; either in the bathroom or outside. If you don't see the actual area, just know there's smoking in the room you can't breathe in and it's either cigarette smoke or marijuana smoke, either way it's smoky.

THE KICKBACK - Kickback's are usually in a house. It's sort of like a party but most likely there is no dancing. Most of the teens there know each other very well and it's like one big social event where you can just kickback and do whatever, which could be listening to music, watching a movie, playing games or more. Everyone is basically just sitting around talking over good music that they all enjoy.

If the kickback is small enough, you won't need a smoking section or beer bong because the majority of people brought their own goodies and are willing to share and most of the time depending on the type of crowd you hang around there is no alcohol or drugs.

THE BIRTHDAY PARTIES – Birthday parties are the type of parties that parents always think are safe. That's because they are...when you're like 12! At that age it's a family party for the whole clan to get together and they actually bring those dumb gifts you hate and are happy to get rid of. But, don't get me wrong, as you grow older and the parents aren't invited anymore;

there will still be those disguised chaperones which is normally uncle Bob or Aunt Anna. An easy way to spot them out is to look for the older person that's either standing around not eating but posing as a fake security guard or the obnoxiously off beat relative on the dance floor trying to look hip and cool. And If you still can spot them; don't worry their face will be lit up when it's time for cake and that's because they're the ones lighting the candles on the cake.

Eventually there will be no chaperones and that's when your birthday party turns into a house party with a purpose.

And lastly let's not forget the religion and culture parties like Bar Mitzvahs and La Quinceañera but those are more for close friends and family and the idea of you turning that into a teen party...not a chance

15

in hell with Grandma and Grandpa dancing to their cultural music of choice.

THE RAVE – Raves are normally big concerts and events where the music is very loud and very retro. Teens are normally wearing lots of colors, with lots of homemade jewelry on their neck and lots of colorful bracelet on their wrist. The sad thing about Raves' is that it's known for sex, drugs, and alcohol. Many Rave goers say it's a lot of drugs and pill popping going on which leads to sex and god knows what else. Needless to say, this is definitely not my cup of tea, but some teens don't share in my thoughts, and that is "OK" with me because I LOVE MY LIFE!

"MY MAMA'S PARTY RULES"

NEVER lie to your parents about where the party is going to be held, because if something bad happens, how will your parents know where to find you.

1. NEVER lie to your parents about who you are going to the party with. Many girls have unfortunately been victims of crimes or have disappeared and their crimes will never be solved because no one knew who they were with or the last person to see them.

2. NEVER go to a party with a boy without telling your girlfriends or your parents. Many girls have been date raped and choose not to press charges because they are either

ashamed to tell whom they were with or just simply scared to tell. Trust your instincts, tell a friend about your date or who you are going to a party with. If you are afraid to tell people who you are going to a party with, then you should not be going at all.

3. If you are underage, never drink alcohol at a party. But who am I kidding, most teens drink at parties so that theory pretty much goes out the window so be a safe drinker if you are going to drink, and if you don't drink, kudos to you! And if you do drink...**You Better Not Drive**!

4. Never let someone hand you a drink. Drinks can be spiked or drugs can be put into your drink without your knowledge. Many teenagers can be drugged at parties for the sole

purpose of sex and other obscene things such as pictures, gags and more. So never ever take a drink from someone, because you will most likely regret it for the rest of your life.

5. Never sit your drink down to dance or walk away and then come back to get it. The same rules apply, it gives someone a chance to slip something in your drink. Trust me it will be safer just to get a new drink in a new cup.

6. Never drink spiked punch, you will never have any clue what type of alcohol was used to spike the punch. Some alcoholic beverages have harsh allergic reactions and can cause you harm or even death.

7. Never become intoxicated at a party! This is not pretty and you won't look pretty either. You will be the

laughing stalk of the party. You may think it's cool, but you will be the most talked about person the very next day as you are puking your guts out on your bathroom floor. And you pretty much can figure out what people will be saying about you, and what's more importantly, do you really know what you did the night before. I don't think so!

8. Never leave a party and drive if you had a drink, nor should you ride with anyone who had a drink at the party. Call a cab, call your parents, or simply ride with someone who is sober. You will thank yourself in the morning. And guess how many brownie points you get from mom and dad if you call them for a ride...zillions! Their trust in you just shot way up. You are now the good

kid they can brag about once again. Trust me as a teen, you're going to need them brownie points because you never know when you will have to cash them in.

9. NEVER go to one party and then to another without phoning home. My mom has the "**ABC**" rule since I was a kid. What is the "**ABC**" rule you may ask? It's simple:

a. Point A is where you are supposed to be

b. Point B is where you go next after Point B

c. Point C is normally where you end up at the end of the night and it's normally not home.

In essence if you arrive at Point A, this is where you are supposed to be, if you decide to go to Point B, and then Point C, you must call home or tell someone you know when you go to other destinations throughout the night.

NEVER keep traveling to different parties and places throughout the night without telling someone. If you are in an accident or a horrible event occurs at Point B or Point C; how will the police or your parents know where to find you if you were supposed to be at Point A?

In my household my mom will do a drive-by and check my points even till today. She still checks on me all through the night via my twitter, phone, or facebook, she always know where I am. It used to bother me, but now, I know I am loved and she cares. I am much more at ease with my friends knowing my mom knows where I am. A lot of my friends think my mom checks up on me too much, but at least that lets them know, you can't do anything crazy with me, because my mom will know, so they too are on alert about their behavior.

So it's ok to party and party hard, you are a teen so go out and have some fun, but be safe, be smart, and definitely be a responsible teen.

Love & Lust!

Those Raging
Hormone's!

Just Remember,

It's OK to Say NO!

Chapter 2

Sex...if you're having it, Be Smart

& if you're not, Kudos 2 U!

SEX! The best way to start off this conversation is to just say the word "SEX" out loud. Sex is not a dirty word, it is the most talked about word in America and the sooner you realize that the better off you will be.

So now that we have gotten that over with, let's start by asking the most powerful question, "Are you a virgin"? If you are, then

25

I applaud you for self-control and your belief in abstinence; but as for me, my answer is no.

Every parent worries about their son or daughter hitting puberty because that drastic forbidden talk about sex will soon have to happen and who's going to talk about it. Most parents are ashamed to, as if they didn't have sex to have you.

I really don't remember my mom actually talking to me directly about scx until after I had sex, but she didn't know then that I was "not a virgin" anymore. So her talk was just a little too late by a few months or so, but at least we did finally have the talk, but if you knew my mom, trust me, she was way too graphic and it almost made me sick. If she had been that graphic a few months earlier, who knows, maybe I would still be a virgin.

Judging from my personal experience with shameful and forbidden sex talk, I would suggest to parents to just hit the question head on and not try to avoid the talk about sex because once you try to avoid the talk or shelter your child the faster somebody else will do it for you.

If they need to learn, let them learn it from you and not from somebody else. Odds are they will see it in school, on the internet, at home, on TV or some other place you don't even want to know about. So just "Do It", talk to your child about it and move on.

The one thing I remember most about the talk was that your parents can't be with you twenty four seven, so you kind of have to make your own decisions and I hope it's the right one. And for the parents reading this book, please know that you will never always be with your child in these situations, so please don't be blinded by your own rules and realize kids will be kids; they have to experience things on their own sometime to learn. As parents, you have to trust that the morals you set in place when you raised them will follow them every day and that they practice a little of what you have preached.

Remember, it goes back to the elementary days, the people who were hands on learners are probably going to be like that for the rest of their lives, and for the other type of learners, all they have to do is see the results of someone else's mistakes or hear a story and they already know what to expect.

I think once you step into having a sexual life as a teen your whole world changes. You start to view people and the world in a different light. For the most part, hormonally you begin to become a young man or lady at a very young age, thus is why I agree with parents when they say, "Have sex when you get older and you can maturely handle all of the possible consequences they go along with having sex.

Most teens don't think about the consequences at the time of their lust for one another. There are many consequences that most teens overlook or dismiss because they think it can't happen to them, such as: STD's, pregnancy, depression and diseases that can lead to cervical cancer or more serious life threatening diseases.

A lot can go wrong in just one try so I suggest practice safe sex at all times if you are a sexually active teen. I also highly suggest that the person you plan on having sex with should be prepared too, and that you both know the consequences of unprotected sex.

As a teen having sex, you have to keep in mind on how you want to portray yourself to the opposite sex, because it's a double standard when it comes to your sexual reputation, and we know "people talk". Your sexual life is never private as a teen. The guys tell their macho experience to their friends and the girls giggle to their girlfriends about theirs. So how do you protect yourself from reputations, you can't, you can't control what people say about you. But you can take caution to not fall into certain sexual categories or stereotypes.

For example: If a guy sleeps with ten girls by the time he turns eighteen he's considered cool or fly but if a girl sleeps with ten guys by the time she turns eighteen she's considered fast and easy or in some cases a "ho" which is a short abbreviated word for whore. In my eyes either way you look at it, having sex with that many people is setting yourself up to be ridiculed by your peers.

So before having sex, ask yourself is it the right thing to do? Do your homework, research your partners background as best you can, and research the consequences of unprotected sex. Because quite simply there is only two routes to take: BE DUMB or BE SMART!

Currently there is a wealth of information out there for teens via the internet, books, schools and more. There are also many free clinics in almost every city that can help you choose the right birth control, the right type of condoms and of course to teach you about diseases. And always trust your instinct, I mean the very first gut feeling you get because if it feels wrong, you can bet everything in life, it is wrong! So don't do it!

Don't just live in the moment of lust or love, get checked after being sexually active for diseases. Getting checked is "**<u>FREE</u>**" at your local clinics so there is no reason not to be responsible for your actions. My mama always told me if you're woman enough to lay down and have sex then you should be woman enough to deal with the responsibilities of becoming a woman and that means taking care of your body and making the right decisions about your life.

32

Having Sex with one partner, is the same as having sex with all his/her previous partners.

PROTECT YOURSELF!
USE A CONDOM!

Also, be careful and take your partners feelings into consideration. Some people regret losing their virginity or at least wish they had waited a little while longer. Honestly after my first time, I was like is this what all the fuss was about, I definitely could of waited until not only I was ready but a bit more knowledgeable, plus keeping the secret from my mom, was killing me. I realized I really needed her, but because she knows me so well, she figured it out anyways and we had a long, long, graphic talk about life and everything else. So now, I'm not that girl in the social group giggling about sex, or saying things I really don't know, now I can have a decent but educated conversation with my peers about the do's and don'ts of teen sex. Because when you are a girl reaching puberty you now have that "v" card (which means virginity) hanging over your head. It's like when you turn 18 and everyone wants to give you a credit card, you just automatically start getting them, it's as if the world knows you are 18. Well the same with the opposite sex, it's like they see your glow and your "v" card from a distance. Treat your "v" card like a credit card, if you would not just give your credit card to anyone or some stranger than definitely don't give your "v" card out. So protect your "v" card as long as you can, it will be worth it in the end.

My suggestion is if you are considering sex or know someone that is, please do your homework. Know these key facts:

1. Know your partner as best as possible.

2. Know the types of diseases.

3. Discuss your "pro-choice" options just in case you just happen to get pregnant, which we all know is not a mistake, because you should know your consequences before submitting yourself to sexual behavior .

4. Know how to use condoms and which one to use.

5. Never be forced to have sex "No means No". If you are forced to have sex, notify your family and the local police department

immediately. Protect yourself and your rights.

So just remember having sex as a teen comes with a lot of pressure and a lot of responsibility.

BE RESPONSIBLE!

Princess Hype is what they called me...
I was just a little bit psycho back then around
age 15, I think? All I know is that I was just
simply hyped all the time, on stage and at
home... thus I earned the name.
But it was a natural high...**NO DRUGS!**

Chapter 3

Drugs...*more than the experiment!!*

JUST SAY NO. That's the first thing parents and teachers say to you about drugs. They don't teach you anything about drugs because honestly they really don't know themselves, which means to learn about them you have to find out for yourself through research or unfortunately you learn from bad experiences.

If you have been introduced to drugs before, you know how it really happens. More than likely you will be introduced to drugs by your friends or peers, or a friend of a friend, which means technically they are not your friend. Either way you look at it, it's someone that you know from your mutual surroundings.

Don't be in denial, drugs do exist and more than often your friends or someone you know are a drug user or has experimented with drugs before.

The first time I was introduced to drugs was when one of my friends was smoking marijuana. I didn't think it was that bad of a drug because the people that I knew that smoked marijuana they seemed pretty normal to me in my eyes. Because of people always telling me "JUST SAY NO", I truly thought only bad people did drugs and that I was going to be condemned forever.

So of course like the rebel I am, I tried it. I thought everyone else is doing it and they seemed to be doing fine to me so it must be pretty cool. I was what they call a social smoker or experimental smoker on occasions when it may have been around me, just trying to fit in at the moment.

I just thought it was a funny experiment, until one day someone that really cared for me told me, "It's not cute when girls smoke, and you don't look cute doing either". Oh my gosh it hit me, I don't look cute, and if you have learned anything about me so far from reading this book, I definitely have to look cute at all times...lol. That hit me like a train and I said to myself, "I'm smarter than this and I should stop and guess what I did within a blink of an eye because I really wasn't a smoker, I just tried it and was trying to keep up with the Joneses, meaning peer pressure can make you do some crazy things.

The best part of not smoking marijuana is that I am in control of my life, I don't stink and smell like smoke, and I don't spend money on that crap anymore. How cool is that?

Marijuana was the only drug I was introduced to face to face but I do know of some other drugs. I did have some pill popping friends too but I was too scared to try that because I heard that some pills make you totally delusional I told myself, "YOU BETTER NOT!" There was definitely no need to do research on pills, I personally saw the results, plus it takes away your self-control, your self-image and your self-esteem. Personally, I like to be in control of my own life as much as possible.

Taking drugs is a very serious issue. My suggestion is not to try them at all, but then again, some people just have to learn for themselves. So if you are one of those hands on learners, please be careful because when it comes to drugs you can lose your life instantly. To help you learn more about drugs and their effects on your life, I have given you some very informative information in the reference section of this book.

I urge every teen to take the time and review each drug and their side effects. You would want to be as knowledgeable as possible not just for your own sake but to possibly help others or a friend in need.

Chapter 4

Love Yourself...*The skin you are in,
is the best place to be.*

FOR THOSE WHO KNOW ME, know that I have high self-esteem and that I do love myself. No I am not conceited or cocky but I am very confident in myself. Some people get conceited and confident mixed up.

Conceited: –adjective

1. Having an excessively favorable opinion of one's abilities, appearance, etc.

43

Confident: – adjective

1. Having strong belief or full assurance; sure: confident of fulfillment.

2. Sure of oneself; having no uncertainty about one's own abilities, correctness, successfulness, etc.; self-confident; bold: a confident speaker.

3. Excessively bold; presumptuous.

My mom is a Hater!

Now I liked this picture, and I thought it was tastefully done by the photographer... but **STOP THE PRESS**! My mom found one hundred and one things wrong literally: from my thighs being big, the size of my knee caps, my stomach had no rips, my make-up, my pose and the list went on. Now thank goodness I love myself because if I had low self-esteem or a lack of confidence, I would of have jumped off a bridge somewhere...well not exactly, but I would still be crying. But I forgave her especially since she's overweight, **I'm just saying!**

Some haters of course like to just say you're rude and conceited when you're really only confident in yourself. What I'm trying to say is that there is absolutely nothing wrong with having high self-esteem and loving yourself.

By loving yourself, you are picking one of the best ways to live. It makes your way of life so much easier because you have higher standards in life and you know exactly what you deserve. Loving yourself also helps you believe in yourself. You always hear people say you can do whatever it is if you put your mind to it, but how can you believe that if you don't believe in yourself?

When you look in the mirror what do you see? If you were to die in the next five minutes, would you say you were satisfied with the way you have lived your life? If you answer is yes, then you're heading down the right track. If your answer is no, then ask yourself what is it that you can change about yourself to answer yes the next time you ask yourself that question.

47

One thing about me is that I believe that other than God there is only one person that can judge me and that person is me. I live my life the way that I feel I was meant to and I don't let anyone or anything bring me down. I know how to have fun and I know how to keep myself happy. What else do I need?

You should think the same way. What else is it that you need? You were born with a specific purpose in life. Yes the doctor helped deliver you but once you were placed on that bed it was now your journey to live not to just exist in the world but to grow up a decent person and find your sole purpose for entering this world. I believe in all my heart I am living my life and following my goals, and finding my purpose.

48

I can't write this book and tell you to love yourself but I can tell you why you should. And even that's hard because I don't know all of my readers personally but I do hope that if you're not in love with yourself already, try it out and see how your day goes. Spend the whole day telling yourself "I love myself" I'm sure it sounds funny, and that's good because it's an easy way to make yourself laugh. I'm laughing just writing this because I'm thinking of you guys just strolling down the street saying "I love myself" or screaming it at the mall. Straight comedy!

Luv thy self, If you don't, nobody else will!

Chapter 5

***Self Image**...*"Life is not about finding yourself, it's about creating yourself."*

Your self-image is who you are and what you portray to others. When you meet someone you only have that first impression to tell them who you are. No one knows you better than yourself so always try to put your best foot forward. Many say your self- image can also be seen by the friends you have or by the people you surround yourself with. Most say you are who you hang around with, so be careful when choosing friends.

Some people feel that because of their physical appearance they do not have a good self-image. They seem to believe that they have to be thin or attractive to have a great self-image. But the truth is self-image has a lot to do with what is within, meaning, believe it or not your beauty and attractiveness should begin within your heart and soul. Yes, self-image is appearance related, but very minimal.

If you think your self-image is appearance related, stand in front of a mirror and take some pictures of yourself or have someone else take them for you. Do this when you looking your best and write down on a piece o paper how you feel at that moment and what you see in the picture.

51

Later take a picture of yourself alone at home when you are completely naked, trust me this works; then write down how you feel at that moment and what you see in the picture.

Once you have done both these exercises, compare your notes of what you have written down, If you feel that you liked the outer self-image better when you were fully clothed and looked your best than you pay more attention to your outer image than you do within. If you felt confident and strong about yourself with your clothing off, than you are definitely a true beauty from within.

Most people need to learn to live and fall in love with the skin they're in. Make-up and clothing should accent your beautiful soul it should not be your complete self-image, it should compliment you only, and not be your entire image that people see within and without your soul. In other words, don't just be pretty on the outside, be pretty from the inside and you will have a much stronger self-image from your very first impression, which will help give you more confidence in your- self than you could ever imagine. You should always want to see yourself as others do.

Remember, self image has a lot to do with the inside, the part that people can't see. This should be your best attribute. You can be pretty on the outside but ugly in the inside. What that means is, your personality and your true self can give you a bad image. For example say you are a fan of a huge movie star that you think is not only beautiful but a great person. But what happens when you finally get a chance to meet that person and they are rude to you as a fan; what becomes of their self image to you now?

So now with all this being said, let's talk about the "Law of Attraction." The definition of the "Law of Attraction" is that like attracts like. If you judge yourself harshly, feel unconfident about your talents, or feel remotely unworthy of love, than, guess what you will attract? People and things in your life are the same. So don't berate your shortcomings, fix them and begin to feel better about yourself so that you can change your pattern of life.

It's almost like the "Wizard of Oz"; sometimes you follow this imaginary yellow brick road going through lots of obstacles and getting off course sometime, but in the end you get to see the Wizard and realize you had the power within you the whole time.

Your self- image is pretty much on the eye for an eye stages. Treat people the way you would want to be treated. Love others the way you would like to be loved as you are creating your self-image.

As for me, people see me the way I want them to see me and people treat me the way I betray my self-image.

So in conclusion, you may ask yourself, how do you get to a place where you love yourself, your self- image, and find inner peace? My suggestion is to start loving you from within. Whether you are fat, skinny, tall, attractive, unattractive, baldheaded, or just not happy with your outer, find that one thing that you absolutely love about yourself and be like a "firework" let it sparkle and shine, make that part of you shoot out your soul like a rocket. Start there and the rest will follow. And most importantly surround yourself as best you can with positive people that support you and love you for exactly who you are.

I personally find love within myself by surrounding myself with love. I stay humble and positive and I am always a great friend. I never bully or try to make someone feel uncomfortable and I hardly ever keep my feelings to myself. I always let people know how I feel and I am always there to listen. I would want someone to be there for me just as much as I would be there for them. Being nice and humble will get you far with the right people. Just stay true to yourself and your self-image will be respected by others.

This is Who I am!

Daring, Fun, Loving, Super Talented,
and full of life.

I value my life, I make every moment count
and so should you!

Until Next Time......Stay True to You!

Chapter 6

The rules of dating*...it's not all
what it seems to be.*

Dating? This is the cross over line where you become a young lady or a young man. This should be an enjoyable time of your life at any age. But before you start to date I think this is something you need to talk about with either your parents or an older friend whom has already dated before. Getting your parents approval before dating is a big plus.

Dating is a mile stone in a girls' life and it's sort of a macho thing in a boys' life. But whether you are a girl or boy it is still an important step in your life and you should be cautious about who you date and especially where you go on a date.

Before I get into my advice on dating, let me tell you about my first date. My first date, well I mean my first "real" date because most times you go out with a guy and it really isn't a date, and that's what happened to me, so my first actual date was when I was 17 years old. His name was Mark J, and apparently he noticed me at a Prom I attended when I was with someone else. Well shortly after Prom, he contacted me via the social web circle and asked me out on a date. First of all ladies, let me tell you, he was the first guy that actually called me and was a real gentleman and asked me out for a date the proper way, and of course I was blushing, so I fully accepted.

Ok now its date night, I smell good, and of course I'm looking fabulous so it's show time folks. He rang and I walked downstairs into a nice black Escalade waiting with the sounds of good music playing, so far so good I'm thinking to myself.

Our first stop was Sushi for dinner where we went to a great Japanese restaurant called "Something's Fishy". Eating dinner here was cozy and fun, but my date started to get a little jealous which was cute, when the cook was flirting with me and of course he served my food beautifully on my plate and Mark's food was sloppy on his plate, now that was funny, but it was all in fun. The restaurant was full and there were a lot of birthday celebrations going on where the wait staff kept coming to sing the Birthday song at different tables. So I said "awe" that's so cute and I told Mark my birthday was in a few days, and before you knew it, he excused himself from the table to go get some silverware, and apparently he went to tell our server to sing Happy Birthday to me, and they did. I was so happy and all the couples around us were saying that's so cute. So it was then I realized I was on a real date, so he definitely scored a few points with me on that one.

After dinner we went bowling and played air hockey and I beat of course; my mad skills beat him at both games. When we were finished bowling I assumed the date was going to end but he suggested we just cruise in the Escalade, listen to music and just talk. So we drove over the Canyon and went to Malibu Beach. When we got to Malibu

Beach we decided to play dare and drive to the top of the spookiest part of the mountain until someone gets scared. No one got scared, we made it to the top, but just as he started to make a u-turn to go back down the mountain, he backed into a tree, now that was scary. Imagine being at the top of a mountain and hit a tree in pitch black darkness, now we were both spooked, but we managed to get down the mountain safely.

Well the night is over and I arrived home safely. This was a great night and Mark J. was the perfect gentlemen. I wish all young girls to have a safe, fun first date as I did. Now if you are wondering what happened to Mark J. the perfect gentleman, well he is still a good friend and he's in College now and I wish him the best forever, he was definitely more than just the normal dinner and a movie date.

Now you know about my first date and yes I have been on plenty other dates since then, some have been fun, some have been an experience and some have definitely been "Hell Date". All in all it's something that every young adult will go through because it's part of the steps to marriage.

But let's talk about my ten rules of dating:

Rule #1: Never talk about your X...Need I say more.

Rule #2: Never go on a date without telling someone who you are with and where you are going. Plus it's a good idea to check in every now and then to let your loved ones know you are safe.

Rule #3: Always have your own money with you in case you need to pay for your own meal, or need to catch a cab home when your date turns into "Hell Date".

Rule #4: Make sure your cell phone is fully charged. You never know when you have to phone home or call for help.

Rule #5: Ladies...DO NOT under dress. You should shy away from overly provocative clothing. You never want to send mixed messages on the first date. And remember "No means No". Meaning have limits of physical affection.

Rule #6: Guys...Be the perfect gentleman plus pick up the entire tab. If you can't afford the tab, then don't ask a girl out.

Rule #7: Keep open the lines of communication. Talk to each other about your relationship and keep it fresh and safe. If you are communicating via the web, cell phone, etc. please be careful about sending provocative pictures via cyber space because some pictures are considered illegal especially if you are a minor and plus you will never know who else will see your pictures.

Rule #8: Sexting...which is the new word for sex via the phone. Many teens are doing this thinking it's harmless, but then again this can end up in the hands of someone else like school officials and perhaps even your parents. My suggestion, just don't do it.

Rule #9: Do not be a victim of verbal or physical abuse. Both boys and girls can be subject to domestic abuse. If you feel you are being abused in a relationship, please tell someone and keep yourself safe. Save your life or save someone else's life if you know of them being abused.

Rule #10: Don't date if you are not ready!

<u>Group Dating: (Dating with others)</u>

Rule #1: Stay with the group, don't wander off. Don't mix with other crowds because this could cause a huge jealousy problem with the others.

Rule #2: Split the bill evenly; don't just pay for what you think you ate. This is a waitress nightmare, plus it shows how cheap you are.

Rule #3: Don't argue with others on the date; don't ruin their night because you are having a bad time. If you don't get along with others in the group, ask your date to leave with you and politely excuse yourselves from the night. If your date will not leave, then take one for the team and hang in there because it's only one night. But if you feel you are in danger, then call home or have someone you know and trust that can get you home safely.

Rule #4: Don't give into peer pressure. If others are engaged in things you are not comfortable with like smoking, drinking, etc.. Stand up for your beliefs and do not engage. You will feel better about yourself in the morning.

Riding with Boys:

Rule #1: Never take a back seat. Always ride in the front seat. Never let a guy or his friends put you in the back seat while they ride up front. Not only is it disrespectful to you as a young lady, but it is not safe. Being in the back seat can be a trap for other things to happen. Be accessible, know how to get out of a car at a moment's notice and make sure you are not in a car where your window and door can only be unlocked by the driver. Ask the driver to unlock the safety locks before driving off. Trust me your life may depend on it.

Rule #2: Know where you are going. Be alert when he is driving, know your way home and do not ever travel in unfamiliar territory.

Partying with your date:

Rule #1: Don't pick up other dates at a party. Stay true to the one you came with. Don't make trouble, be considerate of the others feelings.

Rule #2: Don't leave the party with someone else; that would be very disrespectful.

Rule #3: Don't do drugs or get drunk. You will never know what happened at the party if you have no control of your well being. Using drugs and being intoxicated can lead to big trouble that could possibly be out of your control.

About "Nesa" the author.... Straight up!

**FINALLY THE BEST PART OF THE BOOK,
the "All About NESA" section.**

I guess the first thing you need to know about me is that I have been in the entertainment industry since the age of two. I won a Wal-Mart baby beauty contest because my late uncle Tony put my picture in a huge fish bowl at the local Wal-Mart store in Atlanta for a baby beauty contest. A few days later, my mom was called and I won...go figure, a big ole' fish bowl and me. Feels a lot like Hollywood to me!

So, right after my uncle and my mom went to Wal-Mart to collect the goodies I won, my uncle shortly died by committing suicide over the love of a girl. But from the stories I was told by my family, he loved me dearly and he is still my favorite uncle, why because he launched my career without even knowing it, maybe he knew what I was destined to be when he dropped my picture in the fish bowl.

Right after that, my mom got me an agent in Chicago, and thus I started modeling for regional and national print ads, Billboards, stock photos, and doing commercials. I was literally on a whirlwind in the industry and I wasn't quite 5 years old yet.

But my career really took off when I went to a ProScout event in Chicago. I can still remember strutting down that catwalk at four years old, I was the talk of the show and later received many call backs from lots of agents and managers, which later led me to New York where I modeled for the Wilhemina Modeling Agency. I would go during the summer and I had a blast in New York, I mean it was awesome. I loved sticking my thumb out and hailing a cab, my mom and I walked and walked a lot in NY knocking on doors and it was a great experience and it taught me a lot about working your way to stardom. I really do miss New York, it's a cool town. And just to put a plug in for ProScout, if you ever think about being a star and don't know where to start; google ProScout Modeling Events and get to one fast. They are the best, I been to several events, and even spoke at one event to help others, and I would have to say they Rock!

Well enough about how I got started, let's skip to a huge part of the middle of my short teen life. Yes, I was a Beauty Queen. My Beauty Queen days lasted over five years and hundreds of pageants later. My most prized winnings was always winning Miss Congeniality, I just loved that title, it was so special to me to know that the entire pageantry of girls thought I was the most complete in beauty and friendship with the best personality. I won many pageants and many talent competitions and trust me, it was extremely hard being a black girl in the Midwest doing pageants. It was like one black girl for every 100 contestants, some pageants I was the only black girl there, but my mom found a secret weapon that kept me ahead of the game which you will find out in my next book titled "From Beauty Queen to TV Screen", coming soon!

Well believe it or not after doing hundreds of pageants, I simply went to mom and asked to retire at the young age of 10. Yes, I was so sick of the pageant walk, the fake smiles, the psycho pageant moms, and all the drama, I quit, no more dresses, no more make-up, I was completely done, and I wanted to get back to modeling, acting, and doing commercials, I truly wanted to be a star.

So we set out to set me up for the big time. I took lessons in all the tools of the trade. I started taking technique classes in dancing (ballet, hip hop, jazz, and tap), singing, acting and more. I wanted to be fully equipped before going to Hollywood. It was very important to me to be a quadruple threat because I knew moving to California was going to be tough; so I was off to California.

After a few years of training, my mom and I packed up and left Chicago, Hollywood bound, but first we had to make a stop in her hometown, Washington, DC. In DC we spent a few years building up some cash so we could continue our trip to Hollywood, while I commuted back and forth to New York via bus and train to continue modeling in New York. While in New York, we stayed in Hoboken New Jersey and traveled by train to Manhattan for auditions. Now that was a fun time and I enjoyed continuing my dance training at the Broadway Dance Center. If you have never been to New York, it's just like the Jay-Z and Alicia Keys song, the bright lights will definitely inspire you and the whole city never sleeps, there is always something going on.

So finally the day came when my mom stuffed about $10,000 in her purse she had been hiding and saving and we hopped a plane to sunny California, with a few hopes and dreams and a few contacts we had made. I was young, curious and just a little scared, but I figured I'm rolling with my mom, I got my dreams, we got some money, and so what could go wrong, right? Well lace your boots, a lot went wrong.

Because of all the traveling and working in several different States, I guess some would say we were ready for Hollywood, but oh boy, that was not the case. We came with no car, and that was our first mistake, we thought it would be like New York. So without having a car, my mom and I took a bus everywhere for about six months. I remember having two or three auditions in different locations and we just hustled the metro system, somehow we made it everywhere on time.

I was used to only a few people being at an audition and always having a call back or being booked by the time I got home. But in Hollywood—OMG!—there were hundreds of kids on auditions. And there were no callbacks. The competition was fierce and everybody had resumes as long as your arm. I finally figured out what they meant when they say "You Are Not In Kansas Anymore".

Hollywood bound started to look pretty grim after all those auditions, but then I started to get call backs, it was like, the Casting Directors were starting to see my talent. I remember my first big callback was for "Akeelah and the Bee", I must have auditioned for that many times, but unfortunately I didn't get the role and because of that I never wanted to see the movie. I guess I was a little salty...lol. But, eventually I saw it a few years later on DVD and it was a good movie.

Well from the many auditioning experiences and from meeting other great actors in Hollywood, I strongly started to develop a great respect for the hustle in Hollywood and definitely a total new respect for the

Performing Arts. I was starting to get the hang of what I need to do to make it but my mom was running out of money and getting exhausted with the Hollywood moms and their drama. But we managed to be strong enough to just focus on my career goals and why we flew to Hollywood and things began to get a lot better.

Now that you know the beginnings of my life, let's skip to the middle of my life which is where I am now, an eighteen year old entrepreneur teen that means business. I play hard and I work hard. Thus which brings me to why I wrote this book, my teenage years, OMG, it has been tough, I think I am pretty much loud about it all. I have experienced so much in so little time in such a big city like LA.

Through all my mistakes, decisions, and of course a few triumphs here and there, I consider myself to be a pretty cool chick. I am really laid back when it comes to being a typical teen, but aggressive when it comes to business and my career goals mainly because Entertainment has been my whole life, it is my life!

I am care free, beautiful, confident, and I wear my heart on my sleeve, and most importantly, if I feel it, I pretty much will say it, even though sometimes it is not the best but oh well, we all have our faults.

Now don't get it twisted, when I said I'm beautiful I didn't mean on the outside physical attributes, I mean I am beautiful when it comes to both, my inner and outer beauty, although I may have pimples and blemishes, I don't care, I feel I'm beautiful, so I say it and that is something you have to learn within yourself, because it is never about what others feel, it's about you, which is why I said this is my favorite section of the book all about me, because no one knows me but me.

So go figure my first book and it's about my dysfunctional but fun and accomplished teen life thus far. The only thing I know is, don't make my mistakes, if I can save or help one teen, it's worth the ink on the paper! And no matter what I want to let teens know that if you can dream it, believe it, it costs nothing to follow your dream, just act on what you believe in.

So "Straight Up", I'm a real teen, the real deal, I can relate and I love my life. I love being a teenager and I would not trade in being a teen for anything in the world.

84

My advice to young people is to enjoy your silver years as a teen. Embrace them, make some mistakes, learn from them and move on, but most importantly, live your life, create your own sense of being, and go after every dream and goal you have, just do it!

MY GALLERY OF LIFE:

My very first glamour shots!
Compliments of **"Roy Cox Photography"**
Baltimore, MD.

My very first glamour shots!
Compliments of **"Roy Cox Photography"**
Baltimore, MD

OMG! This photo shoot was the worst day of my life! I was deathly sick with a virus, I had high fever, vomiting, stomach pains and more...I could barely stand up. But time is money so I put on my shades and kept it pushing... then was later rushed to the hospital. I will never forget this photo shoot!

Photo by Phil Orona...www.philorona.com

Having Fun at **"The Real Teens of Hollywood"**
Photo shoot

OMG! I was again so sick at this photo shoot, but funny, I got so many great compliments for this picture. Phil the photographer was a trooper, he's the best, he hung in there with me until the shoot was done and I could go to the hospital...I will never forget this photo shoot!

Photo by Phil Orona...www.philorona.com

Start Your Journal!

List your dreams and Act on it!

My dreams are....

Links

You are not alone:

Suicide Support:

National Hopeline Network (U.S.A.) -
www.hopeline.com - 1-800-SUICIDE

To Write Love On Her Arms (TWLOHA) -
www.twloha.com

Befrienders Worldwide -
www.befrienders.org

When you need someone to talk to:

The Trevor Helpline is the only nationwide,
around-the-clock crisis and suicide
prevention helpline for lesbian, gay,
bisexual, transgender and questioning

(LGBTQ) youth. All calls are confidential and toll-free from anywhere in the United States, 24 hours a day, 7 days a week. 866-4-U-TREVOR (866-488-7386)

American Psychological Association - locator.apa.org - counseling services locator

AAMFT - www.therapistlocator.net - counseling services locator

Befrienders Worldwide - www.befrienders.org - treatment and counseling services locator

SAMHSA - findtreatment.samhsa.gov - substance abuse treatment center locator

SAMHSA - mentalhealth.samhsa.gov - mental health services locator

AACC - www.aacc.net - Christian counseling services locator

National Domestic Violence Helpline - www.ndvh.org - 1-800-799-SAFE

Rape, Abuse & Incest National Network - www.rainn.org – 1-800-656-HOPE National Sexual Assault Hotline

Don't Hurt Yourself... We Love You!

S.A.F.E. - www.selfinjury.com – "S.A.F.E. ALTERNATIVES

Self Mutilators Anonymous - www.selfmutilatorsanonymous.org

There's help... You have a voice... Be heard!

International Foundation for Research and Education on Depression - www.ifred.org

Teen Advice/Support site - TeenHelp.org

The Jed Foundation - www.ulifeline.org

Mental Health America - www.nmha.org

Voice Your Opinion:

On-Air with Nesa - www.onairwithnesa

Protect Yourself and Your Body:

The Chani Girl Foundation – www.chanigirlfoundation.com

Information you need to know:

www.advocatesforyouth.org/
www.iwannaknow.org/
http://kidshealth.org/teen/

Don't be fooled... Get The Facts:

www.cdc.gov in-depth FACT SHEETS
www.stdcheckup.org
www.ashastd.org
www.sfcityclinic.org

www.inspot.org : ANONYMOUSLY tell your
hookups, ex's, boyfriends, girlfriends and
partners they may have been exposed to a
STD.

HERPES information:
www.cdc.gov/std/herpes/stdfact-
herpes.htm
www.ashastd.org/herpes/herpes_overview.c
fm

HPV/genital warts information:
www.cdc.gov/STD/HPV/STDFact-HPV.htm

HPV vaccine for young women:
www.cdc.gov/std/Hpv/STDFact-HPV-
vaccine.htm
The human papilloma virus is associated
with up to 90 percent of all cervical

malignancies and may play a role in cancers of the vagina, anus, vulva and penis.

SYPHILIS information:
www.cdc.gov/std/Syphilis/STDFact-Syphilis.htm
www.stdcheckup.org/everyone/std_syphilis.html (warning graphic photos of symptoms of syphilis) Genital sores caused by syphilis make it easier to transmit and acquire HIV infection sexually.

HIV/AIDS information:
www.cdc.gov/hiv
www.thebody.com
CALIFORNIA HIV HOTLINE: 800-367-AIDS
www.aidshotline.org

SAFER SEX information:
www.thebody.com/content/prev/art6098.html
www.advocatesforyouth.org/youth/health/safersex

Don't be afraid to use it...
It could save your life!

www.ashastd.org/condom/condom_introduction.cfm
www.advocatesforyouth.org/youth...safersex/condom.htm

www.advocatesforyouth.org/youth/...comm
unication.htm
www.avert.org/usecond.htm

THE FEMALE CONDOM:
www.plannedparenthood.org/...female-
condom-4223.htm

CONTRACEPTIVES Birth Control:
www.plannedparenthood.org...birth-control-
4211.htm

EMERGENCY CONTRACEPTION:
www.planbonestep.com/
Or Call: 1-888-NOT-2-LATE

GAY/LESBIAN/BISEXUAL/TRANSGENDER
PEOPLE:
http://lgbthealth.webolutionary.com/
www.shoutouthealth.com/

Hotlines that saves lives:

CDC National STD & AIDS Hotlines
800-342-2437 or 800-227-8922 (English 24/7)
800-344-7432 (Spanish, 8am-2am seven days a week)
800-243-7889 TTY Services (10am-10pm, Monday-Friday)

Things you should know about Sex

Some STDs can be cured, but not all of them.

There are two categories of STDs. Bacterial STDs are caused by bacteria, and viral STDs are caused by viruses. As a result of being caused by different microorganisms, bacterial and viral STDs vary in their treatment:

- Bacterial STDs, such as gonorrhea, syphilis, and chlamydia, are cured with antibiotics.

- Viral STDs, such as <u>HIV</u>, <u>HPV</u> (which causes genital warts), <u>herpes</u>, and <u>hepatitis B</u> (the only STD that can be prevented with a vaccine)—the four H's—have no cure, but their symptoms can be reduced with treatment.

Things you should know about Drugs

***You Just Can't "SAY NO" Anymore...
You Need to be Educated!***

Top 10 Drugs and their Effects:

1. **Heroin** - Heroin is an opiate processed directly from the extracts of the opium poppy. It was originally created to help cure people of addiction to morphine. Upon crossing the blood-brain barrier, which occurs soon after introduction of the drug into the bloodstream, heroin is converted into morphine, which mimics the action of

endorphins, creating a sense of well-being; the characteristic euphoria has been described as an "orgasm" centered in the gut. One of the most common methods of heroin use is via intravenous injection.

2. **Cocaine** - Cocaine is a crystalline tropane alkaloid that is obtained from the leaves of the coca plant. It is both a stimulant of the central nervous system and an appetite suppressant, giving rise to what has been described as a euphoric sense of happiness and increased ***energy***. It is most often used recreationally for this effect. Cocaine is a potent central nervous system stimulant. Its effects can last from 20 minutes to several hours, depending upon the dosage of cocaine taken, purity, and method of administration. The initial signs of stimulation are hyperactivity, restlessness, increased blood pressure, increased heart

rate and euphoria. The euphoria is sometimes followed by feelings of discomfort and depression and a craving to experience the drug again. Sexual interest and pleasure can be amplified. Side effects can include twitching, paranoia, and impotence, which usually increases with frequent usage.

3. **Methamphetamine** – Methamphetamime, popularly shortened to meth or ice, is a psychostimulant and sympathomimetic drug. Methamphetamine enters the brain and triggers a cascading release of norepinephrine, dopamine and serotonin. Since it stimulates the mesolimbic **_reward_** pathway, causing euphoria and excitement, it is prone to abuse and addiction. Users may become obsessed or perform repetitive tasks such as cleaning, hand-washing, or assembling and disassembling objects. Withdrawal is characterized by excessive

sleeping, eating and depression-like symptoms, often accompanied by anxiety and drug-craving.

4. **Crack Cocaine** - Crack cocaine, often nicknamed "crack", is believed to have been created and made popular during the early 1980s . Because of the dangers for manufacturers of using ether to produce pure freebase cocaine, producers began to omit the step of removing the freebase precipitate from the ammonia mixture. Typically, filtration processes are also omitted. Baking soda is now most often used as a base rather than ammonia for reasons of lowered odor and toxicity; however, any weak base can be used to make crack cocaine. When commonly "cooked" the ratio is 1:1 to 2:3 parts cocaine/bicarbonate.

5. **LSD** - Lysergic acid diethylamide, LSD, LSD-25, or acid, is a semisynthetic psychedelic drug of the tryptamine family. Arguably the most regarded of all psychedelics, it is considered mainly as a recreational drug, an entheogen, and a tool in use to supplement various types of exercises for transcendence including in **_meditation_**, psychonautics, and illegal psychedelic psychotherapy whether self administered or not. LSD's psychological effects (colloquially called a "trip") vary greatly from person to person, depending on factors such as previous experiences, state of mind and **_environment_** as well as dose strength. They also vary from one trip to another, and even as time passes during a single trip. An LSD trip can have long term psychoemotional effects; some users cite the LSD experience as causing significant changes in their personality and life

perspective. Widely different effects emerge based on what Leary called set and setting; the "set" being the general mindset of the user, and the "setting" being the physical and social environment in which the drug's effects are experienced.

6. **Ecstasy** - Ecstasy (MDMA) is a semi-synthetic psychedelic entactogen of the phenethylamine family that is much less visual with more stimulant like effects than most all other common "trip" producing psychedelics. It is considered mainly a recreational drug that's often used with sex and associated with club drugs, as an entheogen, and a tool in use to supplement various types of practices for transcendence including in meditation, psychonautics, and illicit psychedelic psychotherapy whether self administered or not. The primary effects of MDMA include an increased awareness of

the senses, feelings of openness, euphoria, empathy, love, happiness, heightened self-awareness, feeling of mental clarity and an increased appreciation of music and movement. Tactile sensations are enhanced for some users, making physical contact with others more pleasurable. Other side effects, such as jaw clenching and elevated pulse, are common.

7. **Opium** - Opium is a resinous narcotic formed from the latex released by lacerating (or "scoring") the immature seed pods of opium poppies (Papaver somniferum). It contains up to 16% morphine, an opiate alkaloid, which is most frequently processed chemically to produce heroin for the illegal drug trade. Opium has gradually been superseded by a variety of purified, semi-synthetic, and synthetic opioids with progressively stronger effect, and by other

general anesthesia. This process began in 1817, when Friedrich Wilhelm Adam Sertürner reported the isolation of pure morphine from opium after at least thirteen years of research and a nearly disastrous trial on himself and three boys.

8. **Marijuana** - Cannabis, known as marijuana in its herbal form, is a psychoactive product of the plant Cannabis sativa. Humans have been consuming cannabis since prehistory, although in the 20th century there was a rise in its use for recreational, religious or spiritual, and medicinal purposes. It is estimated that about four percent of the world's adult population use cannabis annually. It has psychoactive and physiological effects when consumed, usually by smoking or ingestion. The minimum amount of THC required to have a perceptible psychoactive effect is

about 10 micrograms per kilogram of **body weight**. The state of intoxication due to cannabis consumption is colloquially known as a "high"; it is the state where mental and physical facilities are noticeably altered due to the consumption of cannabis. Each user experiences a different high, and the nature of it may vary upon factors such as potency, dose, chemical composition, method of consumption and set and setting.

9. **Psilocybin Mushrooms** - Psilocybin mushrooms (also called psilocybian mushrooms) are fungi that contain the psychedelic substances psilocybin and psilocin, and occasionally other psychoactive tryptamines. There are multiple colloquial terms for psilocybin mushrooms, the most common being magic mushrooms or 'shrooms. When psilocybin is ingested, it is broken down to produce

psilocin, which is responsible for the hallucinogenic effects. The intoxicating effects of psilocybin-containing mushrooms typically last anywhere from 3 to 7 hours depending on dosage, preparation method and personal metabolism. The experience is typically inwardly oriented, with strong visual and auditory components. Visions and revelations may be experienced, and the effect can range from exhilarating to distressing. There can be also a total absence of effects, even with large doses.

10. **PCP** - PCP (Phencyclidine) is a dissociative drug formerly used as an anesthetic agent, exhibiting hallucinogenic and neurotoxic effects. It is commonly known as Angel Dust, but is also known as Wet, Sherm, Sherman Hemsley, Rocket Fuel, Ashy Larry, Shermans Tank, Wack, Halk Hogan, Ozone, HannaH, Hog,

Manitoba Shlimbo, and Embalming Fluid, among other names. Although the primary psychoactive effects of the drug only last hours, total elimination from the body is prolonged, typically extending over weeks. PCP is consumed in a recreational manner by drug users, mainly in the United States, where the demand is met by illegal production. It comes in both powder and liquid forms (PCP base dissolved most often in ether), but typically it is sprayed onto leafy material such as marijuana, mint, oregano, parsley or Ginger Leaves, and smoked. PCP has potent effects on the nervous system altering perceptual functions (hallucinations, delusional ideas, delirium or confused thinking), motor functions (unsteady gait, loss of coordination, and disrupted eye movement or nystagmus), and autonomic nervous system regulation (rapid heart rate, altered temperature regulation). The drug has been known to alter mood states in an unpredictable fashion causing some individuals to become detached and others to become animated.

Glossary for Sexual Transmitted Diseases

Abstinence—not having sexual intercourse

Acquired Immunodeficiency Syndrome (AIDS)—a condition caused by the Human Immunodeficiency Virus (HIV), AIDS signifies a serious weakening of the immune system. Drugs can now delay the onset of AIDS, but many people with HIV still develop AIDS.

Anal Intercourse—sexual contact in which the penis enters the anus.

Anonymous—no information that identifies a person is used. An anonymous HIV test, for example, is one where a person does not give his or her name or social security number.

Antibiotic—a substance, especially one similar to those produced by certain fungi, for destroying bacteria that kills or inhibits the growth of microorganisms. An antibiotic is used to combat disease and infection.

Bacteria—a living organism that sometimes causes diseases. Bacteria are very small—so small that a person cannot see them with the naked eye. Usually, infections caused by bacteria can be cured with antibiotics.

Cervix—the lower, cylindrical end of the uterus that forms a narrow canal connecting the upper (uterus) and lower (vagina) parts of a woman's reproductive tract.

Chlamydia—the fastest-spreading STD in the U.S.; a bacterial infection that infects up to four million men and women every year. Often no symptoms are present, especially in women. Untreated chlamydia is dangerous—it can cause sterility, Pelvic Inflammatory Disease (PID), and increase the chances for life-threatening tubal pregnancies. Chlamydia is treated with antibiotics and can be prevented by avoiding sexual intercourse or by using a latex or polyurethane condom with every sex act.

Condom (male)—a cover for the penis, worn during sex to prevent STDs and pregnancy. Condoms can be made of animal skin, latex, or polyurethane, but only latex and polyurethane condoms protect against diseases. Condoms are effective when used consistently and correctly.

Condom (female)—there is now a "female condom" that lines the vagina, which is worn by the woman during sex to protect herself and her partner against diseases and pregnancy. Condoms are effective when used consistently and correctly.

Confidential—information that identifies a person is kept in a place where no one can get to it. A confidential HIV test, for example, would be one where a person's file would be kept locked so no one could see the results except the doctor or counselor and the patient.

Diagnosis—an assessment of whether a person has a disease, made by a doctor or clinician.

Ectopic Pregnancy—(also called a Tubal Pregnancy) a pregnancy in which the fertilized egg that grows into the fetus attaches itself to the fallopian tube instead of the walls of the uterus. Ectopic pregnancy can be life-threatening. Rates of ectopic pregnancy increase significantly in women who have PID, an effect of untreated bacterial STDs such as Chlamydia and gonorrhea.

Fallopian Tube—tubes on each side of the uterus through which an egg moves from the ovaries to the uterus. Resemble drinking straws.

Genital Warts—(caused by the Human Papillomavirus or HPV). HPV infects between one half-million to a million people each year. There are actually about 70 different types of this virus. Some cause small reddish or pink warts on the genitals or anus. Some of the HPV types also cause cervical cancer. It is important for sexually active women to get a pap smear so that possible signs of cervical cancer can be detected early and cancer can be prevented. Because genital warts are caused by a virus, there is no real cure–the warts themselves can be treated, but the virus still lives inside a person's body. HPV is passed through direct skin-to-skin contact, even if no symptoms are present.

Genital Herpes—genital herpes is a viral infection that can be controlled but not cured. Approximately two-thirds of infected people don't know they have herpes because the symptoms are mild or nonexistent. When present, symptoms of the first infection usually appear about 1 month after exposure and last 2 to 3 weeks, including itching or burning sensations in the genital area, discharge and blisters or painful open sores, and sometimes flu-like symptoms such as swollen glands and fever. "Outbreaks" of herpes in which symptoms reappear and individuals become very contagious can happen throughout an infected person's lifetime. About 40 million Americans have herpes.

Gonorrhea—a bacterial STD that infects more than 1 million Americans each year. Many people who are infected show no signs of the disease. When symptoms are present, they resemble those of chlamydia and usually appear 2 to 5 days after sex with an infected partner. Gonorrhea can cause PID if left untreated.

Gynecologist—a doctor who specializes in women's reproductive health.

Hepatitis B—a viral infection that can cause damage to the liver, including cirrhosis and liver cancer, and may result in death. It is transmitted through contact with infected body fluids. There is no cure for Hepatitis B, but it can be prevented with a vaccine.

Human Immunodeficiency Virus (HIV)—a viral infection that currently has no cure. HIV is passed during sexual intercourse, as well as when HIV-infected needles are shared and from infected mother to infant. It is estimated that 600,000 to 900,000 people in the U.S. are infected with HIV. HIV attacks a person's immune system, leading him or her to be susceptible to a host of diseases and conditions, and eventually progress to Acquired Immunodeficiency Syndrome (AIDS).

Human Papilloma Virus (HPV)—see Genital Warts.

NonGonococcal Urethritis (NGU)— urethritis, characterized by urethral discharge, painful urination, or itching at the end of the urethra. The response is NOT due to gonococcol (gonorrhea) infection.

Oral Intercourse—sex in which the mouth comes in contact with the genital areas (penis or vagina). Many sexually transmitted diseases can be passed during oral intercourse.

Ovary—the pair of female reproductive glands in which the ova, or eggs, are formed. The ovaries are located in the lower abdomen, one on each side of the uterus.

Pap Smear—a test performed on a woman to see if there are signs of cancer in the genital area. A pap smear doesn't hurt, but it can pinch a bit.

Partner Notification—when a person with an infection, such as an STD, lets his or her sexual partner(s) know about the infection so that treatment can be sought.

Pelvic Inflammatory Disease (PID)—a gynecological condition caused by an infection (usually sexually transmitted) that spreads from the vagina to the upper parts of a woman's reproductive tract in the pelvic cavity. PID takes different courses in different women, but it can cause abscesses and constant pain almost anywhere in the genital tract (reproductive system). If left untreated, it can cause infertility or more frequent periods. Severe cases may even spread to the liver and kidneys, causing dangerous internal bleeding, lung failure, and death.

Pelvis—the lower part of the abdomen between the hip bones. Organs in a female's pelvis include the uterus, vagina, ovaries, fallopian tubes, bladder, and rectum.

Pubic Lice—tiny insects that live in genital areas. They are spread through sexual contact, as well as when infested bed sheets, clothing, or towels are shared.

Itching is the main symptom of pubic lice. Skin may be irritated, and a rash may develop from extensive scratching and digging. Pubic lice can be treated with a medicated shampoo.

Reporting—the process of notifying the federal, State, regional, or local database of new cases of infections. This provides a "big picture" so that we can track different diseases.

Scabies—tiny insects that infect genital areas during sexual contact or sharing of infested bed sheets, towels, or clothes. Scabies are mites that cause severe itching. Extensive scratching can also cause a rash. Like pubic lice, scabies can be cured with a medicated shampoo.

Semen—the fluid from a man's penis that contains sperm.

Sexually transmitted disease (STD)—an infection that is passed during oral, anal, or vaginal sexual contact. There are many sexually transmitted diseases, including chlamydia, gonorrhea, syphilis, genital herpes, HIV, genital warts, and trichomonas.

Spermatozoa (sperm)—the male sex cells. Sperm can fertilize an egg during vaginal intercourse and provide half of the information to make a new life.

Spermicide—an agent that kills spermatozoa (sperm). Spermicide can be found in some condoms.

Sterile—unable to get pregnant or get someone pregnant.

Sterility—the inability to get pregnant, or get someone pregnant; often caused by the effects of untreated bacterial infections such as chlamydia or gonorrhea.

Symptom—any noticeable change in the body or its functions that indicates disease; a sign that disease is present.

Syphilis—a three-stage STD that affects an estimated 120,000 people each year in the U.S. The first symptom appears 10 days to 3 weeks after exposure and is characterized by a painless red (chancre) sore on the genitals or inside the vagina. This sore goes away. Second-stage symptoms include a skin rash and flu-like symptoms. These symptoms will also go away, but it does not mean that the infection is gone. If left untreated, syphilis progresses into a latent stage that can lapse into third-stage, or tertiary, syphilis. Complications from tertiary syphilis are severe: they include mental illness, blindness, heart disease, and death.

Transmission—the spread of disease, including a sexually transmitted disease, from one person to another.

Trichomoniasis—an STD that can affect both men and women; trichomoniasis, also known as "trich" or "trichomonas," affects about 3 million people every year. When symptoms are present, the infection results in vaginitis in women and urethritis in men.

Urethra—the tube in the penis that carries both urine and semen.

Urethritis—inflammation (swelling) of the urethra, can be painful. STDs, if they are symptomatic, often cause urethritis.

Uterus—the small, hollow, pear-shaped organ in a woman's pelvis. This is the organ in which an unborn child develops. It is also called the womb.

Vaginal Intercourse—sexual contact in which the penis is inserted inside the vagina. STDs can be transmitted during vaginal intercourse.

Vaginal Fluid—the natural liquids produced inside a woman's vagina. In an infected person, STDs can be passed when vaginal fluids come in contact with the genital area of a woman's sexual partner.

Vaginitis—inflammation (swelling) of the vagina. When symptoms are present, STDs can often cause vaginitis.

For More Information:

Centers for Disease Control and Prevention
(CDC)
1600 Clifton Rd, Atlanta, GA 30333, USA
800-CDC-INFO (800-232-4636)
TTY: (888) 232-6348, 24 Hours/Every Day
cdcinfo@cdc.gov

www.ingramcontent.com/pod-product-compliance
Lightning Source LLC
Chambersburg PA
CBHW032111040426
42337CB00040B/204